We Keep Our Potato Chips in the Refrigerator

WE KEEP OUR POTATO CHIPS IN THE REFRIGERATOR

A Memoir of an Alzheimer's Victim

Patricia Cox

iUniverse, Inc.

New York   Bloomington

Preface

According to a recent statistic from the Associated Press, "More than 35 million people around the world are living with Alzheimer's disease or other types of dementia...Barring a medical breakthrough, the World Alzheimer Report will nearly double in 20 years." These are staggering figures.

"We Keep Our Potato Chips in the Refrigerator" is a touching memoir about Fred Thompson who endured this devastating disease and the reflections of his wife and caregiver, Patricia Cox, who learned through day by day experience how debilitating this unfair change of life can be. The purpose of this book is to let other caregivers, as well as relatives and friends of the Alzheimer sufferers, know they are not alone in their dire situations. Patricia shares candid stories with humor mingled with profound sadness.

Patricia, mother of 3 daughters and grandmother of 11 blessings, is a former teacher for the Denver Public Schools and Cherry Creek School District. She earned her Masters degree in Guidance and Counseling and is currently teaching memoir writing classes for the Osher Lifelong Learning Institute for the University of Denver and The Academy for Lifelong Learning. The reader may expect a few chuckles as well as a few tears from this honest exposure to living with a victim of Alzheimer's.

TABLE OF CONTENTS

Introduction

This is a story of a man and a woman. The man entered that unfair and confusing world of Alzheimer's, and the woman tries to understand this world, but can only view it by his behavior. That man, Fred Thompson, was my husband of ten years. If any of what you are about to read seems callous or insensitive, please know that Fred or any victim of this terrifying disease has my utmost respect. You've heard the well known sentiment that it's better to laugh than cry. I believe it's true, and that humor adds a buffer to life's sharp edges.

In an article by Martha Beck, Polly describes her father's Alzheimer's, "At first my dad wasn't totally out to lunch; he was just…snacking. Then he definitely went out to lunch, then breakfast, then dinner." Martha adds, "Just acknowledging this is funny makes it tolerable.

Cracking up can keep caregivers from, well, cracking up."

Seeing the funny side of any situation was a part of Fred's fabric. He could produce a pun quicker than most people could think of an appropriate response. While I was writing this memoir, Todd and Laurie, his children, each e-mailed me a list of one liners that they knew their dad would have loved. They introduced these puns with "For those who knew my father, these will remind you of his "punny" sense of humor. For those who didn't know him, you should have. He was a great man."

I smiled as I read these groaners and agreed wholeheartedly that Fred would not only have approved of these awful witticisms, he would have improved on them. He would have added more punch (Fred, did you notice the *pun* in *punch*?) to these that would make you smile. I've included some of these puns to begin each chapter to allow you to chuckle or groan before you read about the distressing and tragic progress of Alzheimer's disease.

It's unforgivable to poke fun at a disabled person, but to highlight the levity in the disability, if it is not at the person's expense, is pardonable and, in fact, it is how I managed to get through this frightening ordeal. I have ached for the Fred with whom I fell in love and even loved with my whole being the person he gradually became. Witnessing his slow transition into dementia was painful and lonely. As a consequence, I began to treasure the endearing times when I could smile and even laugh because so much of our lives was spent in uneasiness, fear, unknowing, and in the sadness of this terrible disease.

The Alzheimer's Association has compiled and published a list of ten of the most common warning signs of this dreaded disease. I have interspersed these warnings throughout the chapters, not in chronological order, but as they played out in Fred's life. To my dismay, I discovered far too many examples I could have used to demonstrate these common warnings. I hope the ones I have selected convey the shattering reality of Alzheimer's.

Dedication

This book is dedicated to all those afflicted with Alzheimer's disease and their patient caregivers.

CHAPTER ONE

▼

FRED'S WORLD

*Two cannibals are eating a clown. One says
to the other, "Does this taste funny to you?"*

He walked down the hall and stood at the door to see
if I was there. Once he was satisfied to see that I was
actually there reading my book in the spare bedroom,
he would return to his demanding task of wandering
around the house or perhaps taking a short nap. Then
he would reappear at my door to check again for the
fifth or fifteenth time that autumn afternoon. Since
Fred had diminished short term memory, repetition did

not bother him simply because he did not experience it as such. This was his job, and he did it well. *Number one of the 10 Warning Signs of Alzheimer's is memory loss.*

He would feel relief when he discovered me curled up absorbed in my reading while I would feel a sense of craziness staring at this six foot plus figure popping in the door and then disappearing. *Now you see me, now you don't.*

In my wildest dreams, I would never have predicted that this bright man I met on a blind date over a dozen years ago would become so mentally limited. Alzheimer's stole my soul mate's life and thus took mine as well. Fred would have been mortified if he could have seen how this cruel and senseless malady had changed him. He had told me many times during our early life together that he would never live in a nursing home. His exact words were, "Just shoot me if I can't take care of myself." It was indeed way past time to load that gun, but he wasn't aware of his condition or his previous death wish.

When we first dated, he would look dashing and well groomed in a sport coat and slacks or golf shirt and khakis. I can recall a time when we were visiting Lula, his mother, in a hospital in Pueblo. Dressed in a yellow shirt and light colored jacket, Fred was standing at the foot of her bed with the morning sun shining on him. He was bantering with Lula, who was recovering from surgery, about their upcoming *foot race.* I decided at that moment that the grey templed man with the sparkling eyes was the most handsome being I had ever seen.

Later this same man would go unshaven and unbathed wearing the same shirt and pants day after day. He would be dressed each morning before I could confiscate his dirty clothes. When I could rescue these smelly garments for the laundry, he would choose a second similar uniform and wear them until they almost could stand up by themselves. His minimal wardrobe choices proved to be a metaphor for his life. His daily routine, conversation, and eating habits also shrunk with each passing day.

Alzheimer's disease is a progressive and fatal brain disorder. At this time there is no cure. Recent research yields the following staggering facts: 5.2 million people are living with Alzheimer's; every 71 seconds someone falls prey to this hideous disease, and it is the seventh leading cause of death. Since I am not a scientist or a medical researcher, the only contribution I have been able to make to alleviate this disorder is to donate some time and money to the Alzheimer's Association. While I regret to add those contributions have been minimal, what I have given in abundance is my barrage of petty complaints and a litany of dissatisfactions against The System. *Why hasn't someone found a cure for this distressing disease?*

Yes, I have been a big help. But when you are in the middle of a raging fire, it's hard to think about a fire drill.

During our courting days, I was impressed by this capable bachelor's culinary skills. Fred prepared nothing fancy, but his spaghetti, pot roast, and baked salmon rivaled most meals I fixed for him. So I was saddened when he lost interest in cooking, especially his outdoor grilling, our summer mainstay. I insisted he grill steaks and hamburgers for us long after he knew what he was doing. He would light the grill, put the steaks on and then forget what he was doing. When I would ask him to check the meat, he wouldn't know what I was talking about. *Number 2 in 10 Warning Signs for Alzheimer's is difficulty in performing familiar tasks.*

He began to prefer the blandest of foods. Because he couldn't remember when or what he had last eaten, often I found him sitting at the kitchen island eating his favorite meal, Banana Nut Crunch Cereal. Minutes later, he would top it off with his favorite dessert, Banana Nut Crunch Cereal. A short while later, he would indulge in his favorite snack, Banana Nut Crunch Cereal. He put a few pounds on his formerly trim body, but since he also forgot when he had last walked around the block, that repeated practice kept him more or less in shape.

Fred had a dry wit that made me laugh even when I didn't want to. He amazed me with his puns, the cornier the better. After dementia set in, he still went for the joke, but it lost its cleverness for those of us who had heard it several times daily. And all too often, his attempt at humor would miss the mark entirely. His repetitious patter must have amused him, but it annoyed others.

Every morning without fail, he would say, "Get out of bones you, lazy bed." When I would say, "Good morning," he would answer either "Good afternoon" or "What are you *mourning* about?" I wanted to scream, "I'm mourning the man who used to be my husband!" But, of course I held my tongue.

If I asked him if he wanted some cereal, he would reply, "Why are you so *cereal*?" (I suppose he meant *Serious.*) I'm *cereal* about getting help for you, my beloved Fred.

When I left the house, I could predict the following scenario: If I said "Bye", he would say, "Sell."

If I called out, "Good-Bye," he would answer with "What's so *good* about it?"

"See you later" would get "Alligator." And as sure as Monday follows Sunday, "See ya" would be followed by "Be ya."

He would invariably ask me where I was going when I started to leave the room. If I answered, "Upstairs," he would respond with, "What are you *staring* at?"

You get the idea. But do you get my frustration accompanied by guilt because of said frustration? He was the one with the illness. I was the one suffering. I mustered as much patience as possible to protect his feelings and dignity, but my true self often wanted to go for the jugular. He didn't choose this unfortunate disease. How could I be irritated? I'll tell you: it was very easy. Sometimes I yearned to crawl inside his head to try to understand what was going on in there, or probably more accurately, what wasn't going on.

I wanted him to answer these nagging questions: *What are you thinking? Is the world scary for you? Is it a foreign place? Are you sad? Angry? Confused? Do you know who I am?*

Could it be that none of those questions was appropriate and that he was merely reduced to a simpler more infantile way of thinking? Even though I say that I wanted to know what was going on in his head, I'm not sure I would ever really want to know. I believe that my ignorance of his thought processes was easier for me to accept than the most probable fear and unknown he was experiencing.

Apparently, what was going on in his brain was a lot of death and destruction of nerve cells, or neurons. Approximately 100 billion of these cells connect 100 trillion points. Alzheimer's destroys these neurons like the pine beetle kills pine trees. This is an apt simile since that portion of the human brain is often referred to as a neuron forest. Fred would have been proud of my word play.

▼

CHAPTER TWO

COURTING

When fish are in schools, they
sometimes take debate.

I once taught fourth grade with another teacher and friend, Lynn. She and I had several things in common: a similar educational philosophy, a compatible teaching style, expectations of children as well as the same exact birth date, January 4, 1941. Astrologists might have correctly predicted that we Capricorns would have comparable interests and tastes. In 1990 I was single and frustrated with the men I had been dating. She and her husband Bo met Fred playing golf and later they saw him several times when Bo was performing with his musical comedy group, *The Lawmen*. I believe Fred even took Lynn to her home one night because she was tired and didn't want to wait until Bo finished playing. When I complained to her about my dating life, she suggested a blind date with this likable man she and Bo had just met. I later found out that Bo was more than pleased with this idea of finding a girlfriend for Fred. He said he was tired of Lynn talking about Fred. "Fred said this." "Fred thinks that," quoted Bo quoting Lynn in jest.

We had our first date in that winter. Fred picked me up in a white sport coat, but no pink carnation. However, he was driving his dusty rose Cadillac. We met my oldest daughter Amy and her husband Greg at the Country Dinner Playhouse to see "Jesus Christ Superstar." Fred joined the conversation as if he had been a part of our family for a long time. Then I didn't hear from him. I thought that was strange because we had had a pleasant evening. However, I didn't particularly care because I was going out with two other men. My life was complicated enough without adding romantic involvement. I was a single parent to three adolescent girls and full-time teacher to thirty high energy ten year olds.

After about six weeks he called, and during our hour long conversation, he took pains to explain all the reasons I hadn't heard from him. He had been sick with a bug that had hung on forever, and his daughter, Laurie had married a man named Bob Storie during this time. Still he didn't ask me out. And still I was too busy to care. A couple of months later I was fed up with the two other men.   I called Fred to see if he wanted to go out. He did, so we did. We went to hear some jazz musicians, and over drinks we got to know each other.

Some chemistry must have been bubbling because our frequent dates developed into a regular routine. Weekends and week nights found us going out for Mexican food at the Armadillo, a popular Denver eatery, eating at my house or his, going to hear Bo Cottrell and *The Lawmen* perform, seeing movies, or enjoying mountain drives. I thought he was movie star handsome, but it was his witty sense of humor that won me over. His ironic style was somewhat spicier than mine, and when he discovered this, he had fuel for much teasing. He called me, "Goody" for "goody two shoes" much to my disdain. Realizing I couldn't shake this silly title, I embraced it. "Goody" became my new name.

Needless to say, my cavalier attitude of not caring whether he called or not did change dramatically by this time. In June we drove to the mountain village, Avon, to stay in his time share condo. Fred's best friend, Lee and his wife Marge, rented a unit near us. We went to an Italian restaurant that night. I wish I could remember all the funny barbs the men exchanged all evening.

The next day, Fred and Lee played golf in nearby Vail while Marge and I had lunch in this resort village. Since Marge had known Fred for some time, I tried to pull from her any juicy information about his past. The only thing I learned was that she didn't particularly care for his last girlfriend. I assured her that I didn't like her either---even though I had never met her.

On the way home we stopped at my condo in Breckenridge for the annual workday and Homeowners'

Association Meeting. Fred worked harder than most of the owners. I can still picture him balanced precariously on a ladder cleaning someone's window on the third floor walkway. This was in sharp contrast to a few short years later when the high altitude gave him severe breathing problems. On another Breckenridge trip, he introduced me to a younger version of himself, his son Todd. We met at Mi Casa, a favorite Mexican restaurant of ours which was in walking distance from my condo. Todd was in Breckenridge to meet with a client which was a pleasant coincidence for all of us. Sooner than expected, I began to meet Fred's family.

My dear long time Houston friends, Tina and Tom, visited me the weekend of the 4th of July. I was delighted to finally meet Fred's daughter Laurie when he brought her to join us for a cookout. I remember Tina's comment that little Laurie Storie had the cutest name! I liked both of his children and they made me feel that it was mutual. Fred met my daughters on numerous occasions. They were as fond of Fred as I hoped they would be.

Fred was an accountant for the Denver Public Schools, and I accompanied him on several of his auditing trips to Pagosa Springs, Pueblo, and Rifle.   One that was especially fun took place when he audited the San Luis Valley School District. Rather than staying in San Luis, we stayed at the Hacienda Inn in the art colony of Taos, New Mexico, so I would have something to do. We would have breakfast, and he would drive the forty miles to work for the day while I sat by the pool reading or writing a paper for a class. I would stroll through the art galleries at my leisure. He would arrive back at the motel around 5:30 and we'd go out to dinner. It was a fantasy week as though we were married and on vacation at the same time. He would work all day and I would play. Then he would come home and we would play some more!

We didn't project ourselves into the future. The closest we came to defining our relationship was in terms of eventually living together. Fred talked about renting out or selling his condominium where he lived in Aurora. The collective assumption was that he would move in with me. In the fall of '92, he decided to do just that. He gave away most of his furniture to Todd and to my daughters. I remember packing up his kitchen and being surprised at some of his culinary items, especially the exotic spices. He brought over his enormous desk, a credenza, a television set for his office, his china, a few knick knacks, a few odd tables, and approximately one hundred golf shirts.

That may be an exaggeration; there may have only been ninety-five.

This cohabitation arrangement worked well for both of us, and if it weren't for my grandchildren, we probably would have continued that life style. How could I as their grandmother disapprove of their shacking up with their honey if I were doing so? Never mind the fact that when we did marry, my oldest grandchild, Jamie, was two and a half years old and did not have a live-in prospect in sight.

Those days were delightful, but I didn't realize how short lived they would be. Hints of the foreboding future occurred, but I attributed them to human frailty rather than dementia. One summer evening, we walked to a neighborhood backyard potluck. After we arrived, I introduced Fred to many of couples I knew. I left him to put my dish on the buffet table and stopped to talk to a friend I hadn't seen for a while. It never occurred to me to worry about Fred since he was such a social being.

When I returned to him, he was extremely agitated and angry. He said if I hadn't returned when I did he was going to walk home. His odd reaction didn't compute with the out-going Fred I thought I knew.

Another incident that puzzled me was the night the teachers at Homestead Elementary School put on an old fashioned melodrama. I knew Fred would get a kick out of it because it was so hokey, the kind of corn he loved. I was disappointed and miffed that I could not convince him to come and see me make a fool of myself performing as a swooning maiden. In fact, all through the play I searched the audience looking for him, thinking that he would show up after all. After the performance, Sara and her date plus Margaret and her husband Don , all dear friends, came back stage to surprise me. They wanted to take me out to dinner. I was so touched by their presence because they had made a long drive, and a little chagrin that my own husband who lived two blocks from the school couldn't make it. Again this was not in keeping with the Fred I had married. I now strongly suspect that both of these episodes of Fred's feeling ill at ease in new environments were indicative of early personality changes of Alzheimer's.

CHAPTER THREE

▼

THE WEDDING

An invisible man marries an invisible woman.
The kids were nothing to look at either.

Before Fred and I met in 1990, we each had experienced long term marriages which were ended by his divorce and my husband's death. (Actually we each had had two other marriages which didn't work out: his lasting three years; mine, six months. That's another book.) We each valued our children and many grandchildren. Besides our love for family, we discovered that we shared other significant interests: reading, a desire to travel, and an irreverent sense of humor. In 1993 at age 65, he retired from auditing school districts for the state. Was this a huge mistake? Was he too young to retire?

But he was no longer happy in this job. He had worked all of his life and was ready to have some free time. Did this decision to give up the challenge of daily employment contribute to his dementia? While that may be a valid question, unfortunately, the answer will never be known.

I retired from teaching elementary school at the same time so we could travel and live happily ever after. My youngest daughter Allison, who was attending the University of Colorado, was preparing to go to Austria for a semester abroad that fall. I told her that we planned to get married while she was in Europe. She adored Fred and insisted that she wanted to be a part of the celebration. Ever so accommodating, we managed to orchestrate a wedding in a week. We had already put on the calendar a family going away party for her on the evening of August 26, 1993. Since that was in place, we decided to provide unique entertainment for the gathering, our nuptials. We bought rings and flowers and found a judge.

We said our vows in my backyard officiated by a former neighbor and Justice of the State Supreme Court, Howard Kirshbaum.

Only immediate family was present with the exception of my dearest friend Marje who took pictures and Howard's wife Priscilla who was also a good friend. One of my favorite snapshots was of two year old Jamie pulling long strands of grapevines onto the lawn. His cute, smug expression revealed how pleased he was with his task while all the adults were busy with some ceremony.

Other photographs taken that day also captured family stories. Fred was so proud of his attorney son Todd who looked dignified in a dark suit and tie, with his model-like girlfriend, Sue. His lovely daughter Laurie flew in from Michigan with his grandchildren, Jennifer, age two, and Tyler, three months. Fred was a devoted father and grandfather so it made the event all the more special that everyone in his family could be there.

There were many pictures of my family too.

The ones of my oldest daughter Amy and her husband Greg, parents of the vine master, Jamie, and three week old Haley were full of joy for their new family member. All the pictures of Haley have her baby mouth plugged with a pacifier, and all of Tyler's have a bottle in his mouth. We absolutely didn't want any fussing or crying on that happy day.

Ashley had invited her husband-to-be, Peter, and Allison's boyfriend Kelly was there. As well as all the special people, we had another abundance. We had Hair—teased, tossed, and shining! If we had taken all that crowning glory from Laurie, Sue, Amy, Ashley, Allison, and yours truly, we could have provided full hair pieces for dozens.

That week I had the sales personnel at May D &F Department Store in a dither as I tried on assorted garments for the gala event. What does a 52 year old third time bride and grandmother wear in a backyard wedding? Everything looked too much, too young, too old, or too too. Finally I selected an aqua paisley tea length dress. I can imagine that Fred may or may not have spent an extra minute or two choosing his casual white short sleeve shirt and slacks.

Another cherished photo was of our one-of-a-kind wedding cake. This poppy seed cake with raspberry filling was covered in traditional white icing with pink and white roses with the simple writing, "My's Happy." This was one of Jamie's coined phrases that became symbolic for our family's good times.

I hadn't told any of my Fort Worth relatives that we were married because I wanted to surprise Michelle and Clarence, my sister and her ex husband who had just recently gotten back together. They were visiting us toward the end of our first week as man and wife. I thought I had pulled the surprise of the year when I left a note for them saying we'd return shortly, signed *Mrs. Thompson.* The surprise was on us as well. They had remarried in their own backyard ceremony in Weatherford, Texas a few days before we did. The "My's Happy" suddenly became "Our's Happy" as we four newlyweds drove to Estes Park to stay in a resort by the river.

Fred and I had five compatible years of living and travel before the grim reaper visited us. We often drove to Pueblo to visit his beloved aging mother Lula. She and her son truly enjoyed each other's company. It must have been she who had encouraged his delight in words. When we would leave her, not only did they do the "See you later, alligator," they followed it by their taking turns with "See you later aggravator... coordinator... prevaricator...and...... procrastinator."

When this grand matriarch turned ninety, all who were close to her were invited to an informal barbecue at Fred's cousin Aarion's house outside of Rye, Colorado, just south of Pueblo. This was the first occasion when I would meet both of Fred's former wives: Carolyn, the mother of Todd and Laurie, and Carol with whom he had worked and had been married to for only a short time. Carol and Fred valiantly raised "His and Her" four contentious adolescents under the same roof. Teenagers are known for testing their birth parents at every rite of passage, but for them to have to adjust to step parents at this hormonally imbalanced time does not make for calm waters. I've been told that Fred and Carol also made their rough waves at the same time.

I was nervous about meeting these women who knew Fred and his extended family members better and longer than I had. I asked him what I could expect. He said that Carolyn would be in the kitchen trying to help while Carol would be engaged in lively conversation in the living room. I asked where I would be in all of this. He put his arm around me and said, "Baby, you'll be with me." Do you see why I loved him?

As Fred and I matured in our relationship, neither of these former wives proved to be a threat. I believe Fred maintained better relationships with both of them after they divorced than when they were married. After Fred had Alzheimer's, Carol offered him a job doing something menial, like moving storage boxes in her office building . She had thought it would help him by providing him a reason to get out of the house and into an office atmosphere. Both Fred and I were appreciative of her thoughtfulness until he came home furious. He expected to be paid while Carol thought she was doing him the favor. It must have been humiliating for him when she explained this to him.

Another post retirement job he had was at the *Sharper Image*, a specialty gadget store. He came home proud as a teenager with his first job. There were definite drawbacks for him in this job. First he had to wear a tie, which meant he had to forgo his normal golf shirt and put on a shirt to accommodate a tie. Did these people know what they were asking? The second obstacle was the job itself. Fred could greet people, but could not locate or explain their unique products. And thirdly, he couldn't find his car to go home. I ached for him when I went in to see him. There he was on a ladder *wearing an apron*, dusting shelves. He did not have to endure such degradation for long because he was told they had to cut back employees. We were both relieved when he was let go. The amount of stimulation he might have gained from that experience was not worth the potential risks inherent in that situation

Chapter Four

THE PACEMAKER

Two antennas met on a roof, fell in love,
and got married. The ceremony wasn't
much, but the reception was excellent.

Fred and I had been married only five years when our idyllic world ended and the surreal one began. It began one spring day in 1998. (I say this marked the beginning, but research shows Alzheimer's can begin twenty years before it is diagnosed.) I had driven to the mountains in Breckenridge for the day. Fred was playing golf, apparently by himself, when he must have had several mini strokes. He only recalled getting dizzy and leaning against the club house of Heather Ridge Country Club. Amazingly, (and in retrospect, dangerously,) he managed to put his clubs in his car, drive home, and fix himself a sandwich. The next thing he remembered was that he was lying in a pool of cold Coca Cola on the kitchen floor. Fortunately he had the good sense to call his doctor who told him to call 911. He was taken by ambulance to Porter Adventist Hospital's emergency room.

When I got home, there was a message on our recorder informing me of this dismal news. I quickly drove to the hospital to be with him. He looked so helpless with all the hydrating tubes and monitoring wires extending from various parts of his body. He had other small strokes while he was there. Perhaps the doctors waited too long to put in a pacemaker, but I choose to believe that they handled his situation as carefully as possible. He came home a different man, but only time would reveal how different.

After that "horse pistol" (Fred's word for hospital) experience, personality changes and memory loss came on so steadily and gradually that there was never a time when we could pinpoint the beginning of *Old Timer's*, Fred's clever name for Alzheimer's.

I made appointments with a neurologist and a psychiatrist who both questioned and tested Fred. Their findings were definitely indicative of memory problems, but were inconclusive. Finally we went to see Dr. Alan Lazaroff, a geriatric specialist who had been highly recommended. (Coincidentally, this doctor was the father of a very high functioning autistic child who was in several of my classes at Homestead Elementary School.) I immediately felt that we were in good hands.

Dr. Lazeroff carefully retested Fred , but his repeating the test for the third time did not increase his score. He was told to remember three words: *world, tree*, and *ball* in that order and in a few minutes he would be asked to repeat these words. He then was asked to count backwards from ten to one, not a difficult task for a retired accountant. But he could not identify the current president, day of the week or the season, *In Alzheimer's List of the Ten Warning Signs, disorientation to time and place is number 4.* After a series of relatively easy questions, he was asked to repeat the three words.

Bless Fred. He said that if he'd just known he was supposed to remember those silly words, he would have.

When he was officially diagnosed with Alzheimer's disease, I was both dismayed and relieved. I was dismayed because the diagnosis made his condition real. I could no longer hope his condition was temporary. I was relieved because finally I knew what was going on and hopefully there would be a miracle treatment for him. At the same time, I was apprehensive and terribly fearful about our future. Like most people, I had heard and read so many horror stories about Alzheimer's. I felt overwhelmed with "what if's." What if I can't take care of him? What if he takes a walk and gets lost? What if he becomes violent? Fortunately, all I could deal with was the present and soon that was too consuming to worry about the future "what if's".

With hindsight, I suspect that he was actually misdiagnosed. I believe that he had vascular dementia caused by the oxygen deprivations to the brain during his small strokes instead of the Alzheimer's, but what did I know? And what difference would the name make? His treatment or lack thereof would be the same. He was seen about once a month by the knowledgeable and kind Dr. Lazeroff, but no miracles were available. Fred began to take Aricept, a medication that was supposed to slow down the symptoms, but I could not see any changes in his behavior. I would have to practically drag my grumbling husband to his appointments, but when we got there, he was always friendly and charming to the doctor. However, in time, Fred wouldn't remember who this nice man was.

Fred remained his cantankerous self, but I was helped immensely by Alan Lazeroff. Through his Senior Clinic I went through an uplifting eight week class entitled *The Savvy Caregiver Program*. The term, *caregiver,* refers to those who care for infirm family members at home. Even though there was not a lot of new information about the disease, the material was presented in a way that lent authority to that which I thought I knew. Through readings, movies, and discussions, I was both comforted and made uneasy by the stories shared. The group leader strongly suggested that I attend a support group in my area.

I chose a support group in Greenwood Village Health and Rehabilitation Center, an assisted living and nursing home facility near my home. The discussions at both sessions I attended were monopolized by a few participants. I found the meetings less than satisfactory. I was upset enough by Fred's and my own situation that it did not seem helpful to leave him home alone while listening at length to other people's difficult circumstances. The meeting was from 7:00 pm to 8:30 pm with about a dozen in attendance. The well intentioned leader allowed the first few people who shared their concerns to ramble on about their issues up to 25 minutes. At that rate, only those few would receive help. I dropped out.

I returned to the same group a few years later, older, wiser and far more patient. Surprisingly, most of the same people were there and with the same leader who failed to expedite the sharings as before. But I was in a better place to listen to others and didn't feel the necessity to tell my story. It helped me just to be there. In the interim the two founding members of the group had lost their mothers to Alzheimer's, but they were so committed to the cause that they still actively participated.

I gained much from the group this time around. They encouraged me to take Fred's car away at a time when I didn't think it would ever be possible. This experienced group advised me to tinker under the hood so his car wouldn't start. Fortunately, I didn't have to go to that means. One of the caregivers helped me by sharing she had put her mother in the dreaded facility where I finally had to place Fred. As I will later explain, I had little choice where Fred would live, but she chose this place as the best one for her mother. This certainly opened my eyes and allowed me look at this center in a more positive way. But it was the shared problems, the real camaraderie, the mutual understanding of the complex disease that comforted the members like a warm security blanket.

The Alzheimer's Association not only provides a list of disease warnings, but also offers a list of *Ten Symptoms of Caregiver Stress* which I've listed, followed by my own experiences.

Denial

I thought I was too smart to be in this state. I realize now that for the first few years I was convinced that

Fred was far more capable than he actually was. When he wouldn't do something (mow the yard, shovel the snow off the sidewalks, take a shower), I thought he was being obstinate. In reality, he had little choice. Either he could no longer see the point in performing such tasks or did not remember how. Or perhaps his memory loss made him fearful.

Anger

I was angry that there seemed to be more dollars spent on the penis than the brain.

Where was the comparable memory enhancer like the performance enhancer, Viagra? I was also angry that I was no longer a part of a normal couple who could have folks over for a pot of beef stew or go out to fancy restaurants where clean clothes were the norm.

Social Withdrawal

Oops! My anger runneth over to #3. I was married, but not part of a couple. I felt guilty and worried when I went out without Fred. We did nothing social except family gatherings which had their own stresses.

Anxiety

I wasted time and energy worrying about the future. Should I keep Fred at home? Is there a better place for him? What would his next mishap be? Who was I mostly concerned about: Fred? My daughters? My grandchildren? Me? I was always on guard when taking Fred out. Where is he? What item has he picked up that he shouldn't have? What will happen to this man I love?

Depression

To counter depression, I drank more and more wine. Cheers!!   There is nothing like solving one problem with another.

Exhaustion

I couldn't relate to this one. I didn't have the time or energy to be exhausted.

Sleeplessness

Since I anesthetized myself with wine, I slept. Fred and I had different bedrooms so I would get up to check on him in the middle of the night. Then I would have to read to get back to sleep. Certainly, the quality of my sustained sleep was affected.

Irritability

Now we're talking about my life. As hard as I tried to be loving and patient, every time I found thawed food in unexpected places such as a kitchen cabinet or drawer, I was more than irritated; I was scared and disgusted. When I left my unsweetened coffee unattended and Fred, thinking it was his, would sugar it, I'd snap! Don't mess with my coffee! I attribute the irritability to the helplessness I felt.

Lack of concentration

I found it overwhelming to stay on top of Fred's issues and my own life which included my daughters and their families. My desire to be an attentive and caring grandmother was often interrupted by my concern for Fred. Reading allowed a positive escape venue for me. However, my eyes would follow the words, but my ears were always attuned to his whereabouts.

Health Problems

I adhere to the belief that alcoholism is an illness. So, yes, this caregiver had health problems.

▼

CHAPTER FIVE

TRAVEL

Two cows are standing next to each other in a field. Daisy says to Dolly, "I was artificially inseminated this morning." "I don't believe you," says Dolly. "It's true; no bull!" exclaims Daisy.

Once or twice a year Fred and I visited my extended family in Texas. One memorable trip was to Lake Travis where we met my siblings and their spouses: Michelle and Clarence, Billy and Linda, Peggy and Dale. This was the only trip my sisters and brother ever went on with our significant others. We spent an enjoyable weekend in lovely condos overlooking this Texas size lake. The four couples shared an expansive deck which apparently had also been rented to a plethora of cats who entertained us as much as the Broadway musical, *Cats,* without the music. On that Saturday we drove to Lake Buchanan and boarded a triple deck sight seeing boat. We embarked on a three hour "Vanishing River Cruise" which touted the sighting of bald eagles. We all sported binoculars while spotting gulls, hawks, vultures, and wild turkeys. The running joke of this clan was claiming to see the eagles which no one did. Couples on the third deck of our river cruise vessel would run to the bottom deck shouting that they had seen them and vice versa. My family never lets a joke die. After the trip we sent fake pictures to each other of eagles we supposedly had taken on the trip. This was Fred's kind of fun; he loved this hoax.

I'm convinced that it takes an intelligent and patient traveler to untangle the complex web of trading in order to fully utilize one's Time Share. In his better days, Fred managed this ordeal without rancor for destinations for us in Seattle, Boston, Fort Lauderdale, New Mexico, Arkansas, and the Bahamas. This last trip was especially meaningful because we were accompanied by his children, Todd and Laurie; their spouses, Sue and Bob. This was Fred's Christmas gift to all of us. We shared grocery shopping, meal preparation, playing board games, eating out, and much laughter. Not long after that, he planned our two week trip to Australia which was no small task. So when travel became a challenge for him, it became a challenge for both of us.

In February of 1998, we were both excited about our trip with other University of Denver Alumni to the Panama Canal. This took place before his mini strokes and pace maker, but looking back, changes were already taking place in my dear spouse. We sat with the Vi and Lowell from California; Dick and Jan, and Bob and Joy from Denver. Every night there was merriment about strategies for *stealing* the china and silver for my daughter Allison's impending wedding. "Take this elegant serving spoon. It will fit in your purse." "I'll grab these salt and pepper shakers. She'll need these," could be heard from our table amidst the guffaws of laughter. This would have been fodder for my comic husband, but he sat quietly while we dominated the conversation. *In the 10 Warning Sign List, personality changes is number 9.*

At every port of call there was an opportunity to go ashore for a tour. These were pricey excursions, but compared to the cost of the cruise, it seemed wise to take advantage of these sights we would never have the chance to see again. I signed up for every one while Fred remained on the ship. This unusual behavior should have been an alert to me because the man I married would not have missed these adventures. Denial and I were becoming close friends.

In May of the same year, 1998, a few months after Fred's pacemaker was put in, my daughter Ashley and her husband Pete graciously invited us to accompany them and their two babies, Matthew, sixteen months, and Sarah four months on their vacation to St. Thomas and St. John's Islands in the Caribbean. (I'm not certain if we were brought along as nannies or guests, but it didn't matter. I was thrilled we were included.) I was convinced Fred should have healed by then, but he did not share my humble opinion.

My six foot seven inch son-in-law couldn't fit in the normal cramped airline seats so he sat in the bulkhead. This young family was traveling on a shoestring; no seats had been purchased for the little ones. Airline rules permitted only one infant in a row, so Ashley sat across the aisle with one child and Fred and I had the other baby. Or rather, *I* had the other baby. Therefore Ashley and I were constantly wrestling with and trading Matthew and Sarah across the aisle. Fred refused to give us a break by holding one of the twirling dervishes, even for a minute. When we arrived at the posh Marriott Hotel, (paid for by points from Pete's business travel) Ashley and Pete resembled pack horses schlepping all the luggage plus Sarah while I carried dead weight Matthew who finally went to sleep. Fred managed to carry his light weight wind breaker. This was so uncharacteristic of my usually thoughtful husband.

We had a glorious time sightseeing and lolling in the sun, but corralling, containing, and entertaining the kiddos was a job. Fred and I would usually eat an early dinner with them. Ashley would put them to bed with the plan that we would baby sit while she and Pete had a leisurely late meal. The former Fred would have gladly helped with this task, but not this emerging man. He would go to bed in our room while I stayed with the children. His inability to help out made no sense to me.

This was the very same man who, when each of his grandchildren was born, flew to Michigan to take over all household chores while his daughter was in the hospital. He cooked, did the laundry, and kept the older toddler, Jennifer, when Tyler was born. And when Laurie and Bob would go on vacation, he and I would stay with the children, but he didn't need me. He was the grandpa who could do everything from folding clothes, wiping noses to swinging swings. What happened to him?

Back to St. Thomas: Often we would explore the island in our rental car. I should have suspected that something was amiss with my normally witty husband when he repeated the same unfunny comment every time we saw a rundown shanty (which was often), "Look at that mansion." I didn't scream at this stranger sitting next to me in my husband's body, but I felt like it.

▼

CHAPTER SIX

FRED'S PAST

*Did you hear about the thief who stole
a calendar and got twelve months?*

Until we moved Lula, Fred's mother, to a nursing facility in Denver so we could be close to her, we spent many days driving the two hour trek to Pueblo to visit her. This journey always brought back fond memories for Fred. Since I was enormously curious about his past and he loved to tell old stories, his reminiscing was entertaining for both of us. The stories changed over the years and while the most recent recounts are

less accurate, they are dominant in my mind. Because
of this, his true history is sketchy at best. Fred Wilbur
Thompson was born in Vineland, Colorado, just
outside of Pueblo on March 25, 1929 to Tom and
Lula Thompson. Tom was a farmer who had been
married first to Claudia. She died leaving him two sons
to raise, Lowell and George. Tom married a much
younger Lula to help him with this task. They had a
daughter Kathleen and a son Don several years before
they had Fred. In fact, the span between Fred and his
siblings was too great for him to have had close ties
with them.

He vividly recalls that his father was an undemonstrative
man except when it came to venting about his wife's
church, the Seventh Day Adventist. Fred remembered
his lively swearing, "If they (Germans? Japanese?) bomb
the United States, I hope the first place they target is
that GD church!" I think that was meant in jest, but
I'm not sure. Apparently Lula spent a lot of time there.
Fred even attended a parochial boarding school during
his middle school years until he was kicked out for
sneaking off campus one too many times.

Fred recounted the story of his horse running him into a tree after being reigned in too quickly, resulting in small scar in his eyebrow. (Fred's, not the horse's) He told often of his dog who he claimed dug a trench around an out of control campfire, saving their farm's destruction. He had a pet raccoon that his father sold when they needed the money. Fact or fantasy, he was a compelling story teller.

One tale he later loved to embellish had to have come straight from a comic book he read or perhaps a Charlie Chaplin movie. He and his constant companion Alzheimer bragged that he rode down Pike's Peak on a shovel when he was young. Apparently, he must have enjoyed telling this story because he repeated it often. Sometimes he would ride his shovel on railroad tracks, and sometimes he would dodge boulders on his way down the mountain. How does one respond to that? I uttered an occasional "Oh my!"

After Fred graduated from high school he was engaged to a local artist, Shirley Somebody, whose family was quite prominent. She painted a portrait of him that hung in his condo and later in his nursing home room. Why they broke up remains a mystery, but he heard from her over the years. After his death, she sent him a note saying she had moved to New Mexico and would like to see him if he ever got there. I sent her a note informing her of his death and enclosed his Memorial Service program.

Fred worked in a copper mine in Utah with his much older half brother, Lowell. He worked at the steel mill in Pueblo for a while. For three years he served in the Navy during the Korean War and was stationed in Hawaii and Japan. His official title was the paymaster who handled the sailors' paychecks. He said he made enough playing poker to buy a convertible which he sold at a profit before he returned home. In going through his boxes and files after his demise, I found beautiful large prints of two Oriental beauties with fond notes to Fred on them. Always the lover!

Upon returning to Pueblo, he married Carolyn who worked as a nurse in Pueblo. They moved to Denver where Fred attended the University of Denver to become a certified public accountant. He worked for Arthur Anderson and other firms before he began his career as an auditor for the state. Carolyn gave birth to Todd in 1959 and Laurie in 1961.

When the children were school age, their parents bought a boat and house trailer to use in Grand Lake. They sold their house in Denver, and Carolyn and the children spent one whole summer there while Fred commuted there every weekend while living in an small apartment in Denver where he was working. He never spoke of this time without mentioning that Carolyn was extremely unhappy because she was convinced that he was having an affair in Denver. Fred admits that he worked too many hours and wasn't the family man that he later became. I'm assuming the rocky marriage was taking its toll on Carolyn. She took an overdose of pills and was rushed to the emergency room. She was hospitalized and eventually placed in Fort Logan Mental Hospital for rest and evaluation. Fred hired a grandmotherly woman, Mrs. Simpson, to care for the Todd and Laurie, the house, and the meals. She continued to help the family long after Carolyn came home.

Sometime later, Fred met Carol through their work together with United Way. They became friends, and she became his needed support with his troubled home life. Eventually she gave him the advice he was looking for. She told him that now there was one sick person (Carolyn) and if he stayed with her, there would be four (Carolyn, Fred, Todd, Laurie). He moved out giving the children the choice which parent with whom they wanted to live. Todd chose Fred while Laurie feeling protective of her mother, chose her. Later, Laurie overheard a relative saying that she hoped Laurie would not turn out to be like her mother. That was all it took for Laurie to move in with Fred.

I am unsure of the timeline, but in time Carol and Fred married. (Small world indeed: Clarence, the minister who performed their service was my pastor. It was at about this same time that he officiated at the Memorial Service for my husband, Jim, his brother Tom, and his parents, all killed in plane crash piloted by Jim. Years later Clarence was the minister both of my older daughters chose for their weddings.)

Carol and Fred bought a large home to accommodate her two children, Kathy and Grant and his two, Todd and Laurie. Even the most intact families have shaky episodes during the raising of adolescents. I can imagine that this phenomenon was exacerbated with the mingling of two sets of unrelated teens, each having a birth parent and a step parent in the mix. Laurie and Carol got along like lighter fluid poured on hot coals. Fred and Carol's strong personalities found harmony impossible with so many issues facing them: parenting four hormonally active teenagers, their dual careers, and whose money paid for what leading the list. The tension was so great between Laurie and Carol that way too young Laurie moved out into her own apartment. And after three years of trying to fit together, Fred and Carol divorced.

Some sunshine came out of this storm.

Laurie and Carol made amends and became good friends. So did Fred and Carol after the clouds cleared. Kathy had bonded with Fred, remained close to him, and called him "Dad" until the end. Fred and I attended her wedding and later we would enjoy visiting her and her family in Ft. Collins.

▼

CHAPTER SEVEN

LIFE GOES ON

A group of chess enthusiasts checked into a hotel and were standing in the lobby discussing their recent tournament victories. The manager asked them to disperse. "But why?" they asked as they moved off. "Because," he said. "I can't stand chess nuts boasting in an open foyer."

I hope that I have not painted a totally dismal picture of my noble and decent spouse. Let me brighten this canvas. Before dementia Fred was a beautiful person inside and out, but not perfect by any means. He was just so charming, he made you think he was. He was attentive and thoughtful to his aging mother, Lula, his children and grandchildren as well as my children and grandchildren.

Once when Fred's daughter and son-in-law, Laurie and Bob Storie, and their children Jennifer and Tyler arrived from Michigan, they were piling out of the car, when my three year old grandson, Jamie, greeted them warmly with, "Hey, Jennifer, (who was also three,) have you met my good friend, Pa Fred?" Fred indeed was his good friend as well as Jennifer's grandfather.

I recently asked my middle daughter, Ashley, what she remembered about the good days with Fred. Her response was, "Oh Mom, don't you remember how I would tag along on your dates? I was going through my terrible divorce and Fred always included me when you two went to special restaurants. And he would always balance my checkbook. He would balance it, and few months later he would have handle the awful mess all over again. He was so patient and kind about it."

When he shopped for Christmas or birthday gifts for his children, he was incredibly thoughtful. When Laurie said she needed a certain type of dress, he carefully studied the selections in several stores and chose more than one to send to her. This generous gesture pleased her immensely. In contrast, I have rarely bought an item of clothing for any daughter of mine that she didn't promptly return. (This is a reflection on me, not my daughters!) And the gifts and cards he gave me spoke volumes of his feelings which he could not easily put into words.

He taught me to play golf. Well, that's a bit of a stretch. He *tried* to teach me to play golf. We took several weekend golfing trips with friends Lee and Marge . Fortunately, Marge wacked the ball with the same inconsistency as I did so we were a perfect foursome, like a car with two flat tires. But we had much fun because Fred and Lee kept up a nonstop comical dialogue. The men never wrote down our scores and to show our gratitude, we picked up our balls often to keep up with their pace. Sadly, after Fred's affliction, we didn't see our good friends. I'm sure they felt uncomfortable with this new man with whom they no longer could share a laugh and frankly did not know.

When we weren't traveling, our lives took different directions. I filled my days with a variety of activities: babysitting, bridge, substitute teaching, volunteering, lunches with friends, and fussing about the house. As time went on, Fred played golf alone most of the time. He would simply walk on the course, play a few holes and come home. I found out later that he wasn't paying his country club dues, so he was actually sneaking on the course. He had been an avid mystery reader, but one day that was no longer possible. He could not follow the written word. He watched a lot of television, but I believe this activity led to sleep rather than engagement. *The tenth warning sign of Alzheimer's is loss of initiative.*

I was feeling a bit fragmented and less than satisfied with retirement. I had volunteered my time at Wellshire Presbyterian Church recording Sunday's worship attendance and telephoning ill, bereaved, or hospitalized members for their Concern Center. Both of these jobs fell under the job description of Libby, the Parish Coordinator. When I learned that she was retiring, I applied for and got her full time position.

This brought more fulfillment to me and less to Fred who now was left alone much of the time. I came home for lunch almost every day to check on him. I rationalized that I was out and about most days anyway so my working was not much of a change for him.

When Fred was approaching his 70th birthday, I wanted to do something special to commemorate the event. It could have come and gone and I don't think he would have noticed. I decided a surprise party with just a few close friends and relatives would be appropriate. I don't know who I thought I was fooling because I could have told him about the party every day before the gathering and it still would have been a surprise to him. But I went through the motions of preparing the food and hiding it in the refrigerator in the garage. I wanted him to be surrounded by loved ones. I wanted him to enjoy this milestone. I wanted a normal birthday celebration with candles, laughter, and good feelings. Clearly I was in full time denial mode when planning this gala event.

I sent out the following invitation:

Fred is approaching an important birthday.

Which one, I'll decline to say.

He doesn't know a party will take place.

Please come to witness the look on his face.

We will all celebrate; no gifts are allowed.

Special friends are invited, not a big crowd.

I don't think anyone was pleased with my efforts. Having lost his knack for kidding people and making them feel welcome, Fred seemed strained to make small talk with his guests. Most of the people had only one thing in common; they all knew and loved the honoree who was anything but the life of the party. His guests wanted to connect with the Fred they remembered, but that was not possible. I felt bad for the ones who had driven from Pueblo and Colorado Springs for this fiasco. They ate, drank, sang "Happy Birthday" and left.

Fred was not aware of the hours I spent in preparing the turkey, meatballs, cheese, fruit and veggie plates, cake, but what impressed him the most was how all those nice people knew to come. What did I expect would happen? Did I think a festive occasion would bring my old Fred back? Sometimes my thinking was as warped as his.

Fred's memory was worsening, but he adapted strategies to help him with some situations. He would always pretend he knew someone, but after a warm greeting, he would have nothing else to say. He called all the grandchildren, "Tarzan," both boys and girls. And because he always referred to them with that familiar name, they felt he knew them. To Amy's children, whose blond hair was the color of corn silks, he would repeat, "Where did you get that pretty red hair?" They became frustrated after hearing this question a cajillion times, so I coached them to simply answer, "Target." This response pleased them and him a cajillion times.

One evening when I was babysitting Matthew, I decided to take Fred and him to the Black Eyed Pea for dinner. The males sat next to each other on one side of the booth, not a good plan. Before our food arrived, they were engaged in a straw battle. They were blowing wrappers at each other, causing much noise and commotion. I said in my grandmother-teacher voice, "Fred and Matthew, stop that right now!"

Fred looked at me as innocently as his young cohort sitting next to him and said, "*He* started it!" as if they were the same age, six!

As Fred's Alzheimer's progressed, so did many other health issues. He complained of various ailments all the time. Naturally I took each one of these seriously and made appointments with the appropriate doctor. In retrospect, I can see that many of these appointments were unnecessary, but at the time, I didn't think I could take a chance. I am not saying that Alzheimer's and hypochondria necessarily go hand in hand, but in Fred's case, I suspect so. A 2000 calendar was filled with the following: six visits to the urologist; two to neurologists; many to a cardiologist for checkups and echo cardiogram; several for evaluations of potential skin cancer at the dermatologist; nose and throat specialist for dizziness and inner ear test; primary care taker for chills down left side, and more appointments with more physicians for reasons I did not write down. He seemed fixated on not feeling well. Could it be that his brain had so little activity that the slightest pain became exaggerated? One doctor told Fred, "You keep coming up with ailments and I'll keep coming up with solutions." Fred took this advice to heart. (No pun intended!)

▼

CHAPTER EIGHT

MORE TRAVEL

When a clock is hungry, it goes back four seconds.

I had worked at the church for several months when Jerry McCollum, the choir director, approached me with an offer I couldn't refuse. He said if I would join the choir, I could sing with them in the four Scandinavian capitals on their choir trip the following summer. He didn't even know if I could sing and frankly, I didn't either. But I fooled him and the other choir members enough that I joyfully rehearsed their songs and scales until departure time. Of course, I invited Fred, and so we went.   As a bonus we toured England before boarding the luxurious Royal Princess Cruise Ship to begin our journey.

The second night at sea was designated as formal dining. I was certain that all cabin mates who shared our floor could hear Fred's swearing when I handed him a dress shirt, tie and suit. You would have thought that I had asked him to wear a pink tutu and ballet slippers.

"I'm not going to wear a f------- suit," he ranted.

"Fred, you'll look so nice and all the men will have on suits. Some will even wear tuxedos," I pleaded.

"That is so GD stupid."

This argument ensued every formal night, but he always relented. And when both of the single women at our table commented on how handsome he looked, he beamed. I wanted to beam him!

Another significant difference in Fred showed up on this trip. He would not initiate or participate in social conversation unless he was specifically called on to do so. I can recall our trip to Australia before his illness that he was chatting with everyone he came in contact with. I remember wondering why he got so involved with people he would never see again. It never occurred to me that he was simply enjoying these folks while I sat with my nose in a book. But even though we sat with the same people every night on the cruise ship, he would only respond to questions directed to him.

The two week cruise through Norway, Denmark, Sweden, and Finland followed by stops in Poland and Russia went amazingly well, although I attribute it mainly to the grace of God and good karma. Whether the choir was rehearsing and singing in a small village chapel or a large metropolitan church, Fred was left on his own to be a part of the audience. He could have wandered off, but thankfully he didn't. When we were in a crowded outdoor mall area in Gdansk, Poland, my friend Mary and I tied balloons on Fred's and her husband Marvin's wrists so we could keep them in sight. (Marvin had been brain damaged in a snowmobile accident.) We returned safely, and I happily labeled the trip a success although my criteria for such a judgment was gradually being lowered.

His dementia was progressing, but I was in greater denial as to its severity. So in a brilliant move, I opted to sign us up with former neighbors, Ben, June and Catherine for a trip to Spain the next March to visit the Paradors. These were formerly historic buildings that had been converted to hotels. What an ingenious idea! The tourists now pay for the maintenance of Spain's former monasteries and museums. This trip proved to be frustrating for both Fred and me. For all he knew, we could easily have been in downtown Denver. Whenever possible he would stay on the tour bus, sleeping while we explored the sights. When he did accompany us, he would stroll at a snail like pace while our group walked briskly to keep up with the guide. Keeping Fred and the group in sight was an impossible feat as the distance between them was widening with each step. Did I want to be lost in Madrid with Fred or secure with the group without him? I'll never know how I managed to arrive at the right church or museum with Fred in tow. Of course, once we reached our destination, he would refuse to go in. (It's interesting to note, as I'm writing these words, my heart is pounding as it did in Spain when I was in such an anxious state over his safety.)

The most traumatic event took place as we were leaving Spain to return home. Fred had been given his airline ticket, but did not have it as we were ready to get on the plane. Most of our group had already boarded when this disaster occurred. I remember feeling very alone in this dilemma of searching for his ticket. I retraced our steps and canvassed the waiting area. No one associated with the airlines seemed to care. No ticket, no flight! Did they realize I was traveling with a disabled man? Finally, at the last minute, Fred pulled the ticket out of a pocket I had repeatedly searched. *In Alzheimer's 10 Warning Signs, misplacing things is number 7.*

While I was experiencing Fred's progression into dementia, I grieved continually. This grief process includes denial, bargaining, anger, sadness, and acceptance. I spent a lot of time in the first two stages. In order to go on with my life, denial and bargaining gave me hope. Because I was not aware I was using these strategies, it became a pattern to deny Fred's real condition and bargain outrageously that we could travel abroad together.

My sincere apologies go to all the travelers on the tour because I'm certain Fred's behavior concerned them. But most of all, I'd love to tell Fred how sorry I am for my poor misguided judgment in putting him through such an ordeal. Fortunately, for him this memory did not haunt him as it has me. (My heart beat is slowly returning to normal.)

Chapter Nine

The Lasts

I went to a Seafood Disco last
week and pulled a mussel.

I thought that a simple car trip would be good for us both. And it would have been had I planned a reasonable one. Visiting my family in Fort Worth, Texas would have been enough of a challenge, but I pushed it all the way down to the Gulf of Mexico to see more relatives. That was the beginning of all the *lasts*. I didn't know at the time that this was Fred's *last* long car trip. I drove the entire trip while he quoted gas prices to me over and over and over.

"There's $1.82, over there a $1.79, and hey, $1.85, that's the lowest yet! It is so stupid that they have different gas prices.

STUPID! STUPID! STUPID."

The *last* movie he went to was *Fantasia* shown on the giant three story screen. This was a celebration for my granddaughter Holly's birthday. He stormed out of the theater saying it was STUPID and TOO LOUD.

Then there was the *last* time he paid for a meal at a restaurant. Fred had always been frugal, but before *Old Timer's*, he had always been fair with his funds, paying for some of the groceries, meals out, gifts for me and his children. The disease turned him into a miser. We never joined our assets. I paid my bills; he paid his, or at least he paid the ones he liked. The rest he threw away. When we went out to dinner, due to both of our small appetites, we would often split an entrée. He would always say, "I'm not hungry. Order what you want and I might have a bite of yours." This freed him from paying any part of the bill, even though when I split the meal, he would devour the heavier portion.

The *last* car drive to the mountains was also STUPID. His daughter wanted to take him to into the hills thinking he would enjoy it. We drove to Breckenridge where we had spent many days and nights.   I suspect when he was uncomfortable with unfamiliar surroundings, anger was the masking emotion over his fear. We returned home as soon as it was apparent that he was not adjusting to or tolerating this trip.

I pushed travel one more time thinking it would be his *last* plane trip to visit his daughter Laurie in Michigan. I knew it would be important for her. We had visited her family faithfully once or twice a year and I had been concerned that it was now or never to make such a trip. Laurie was so looking forward to our coming so I proceeded ahead with only mild worry. It didn't surprise me that Fred would not pack for himself. But he was adamant while I was filling his suitcase that he wasn't going anywhere. I managed to get him in the car, and all the way to the airport he reminded how stupid this was.

We parked, and he followed me grumbling all the way to the terminal. I dragged both of our wheeled suitcases to United Airlines Ticket Counter and seated him in the waiting area. I assured him that once we got on the plane, we would eat a nice meal and be in Michigan in no time. (Liar, liar, pants on fire!) It didn't matter that I lied; he wasn't going anywhere anyway.

Nervously I stood in line while keeping my eyes beaded on him when it finally dawned on me that he was not going to budge. After prideless pleading, endless cajoling, and coaxing, I asked him if he wanted to go home. His response was, "Let's get the hell out of here." Swearing was one thing he had not forgotten. I could feel Laurie's deep disappointment when I had to call her to say that we weren't coming.

Fred, a former CPA, had always been vigilant about paying his bills on time. We kept our finances separate so I don't know when the *last* time he tended to that task. When I began noticing collection agencies sending him mail, I began to smell a non bill payer. I couldn't convince him that paying bills was much preferable than ignoring them. Finally his son Todd came over, had him sign several checks, and cleared his record.

Poor judgment is number 5 in the 10 Warning Signs for Alzheimer's. I became the accountant's accountant.

Fred was taking several prescription medications, mainly for his heart and cholesterol, which he meticulously put in his M-T-W-Th-F-S-S divided containers to be sure that he took them daily. He had handled this routine for so long that I didn't think I needed to intervene. Then came the day when he was looking at the newspaper and said, "Why does this paper say that it is Monday when it is Thursday?"

I glibly answered, "Because it is Monday, not Thursday."

"No, it's Thursday. I just took Thursday's pills." So that was the *last* time he medicated himself. But the saga doesn't end there. He was determined to handle his own medications even though I tried to convince him that I wanted to help him. When he couldn't find his meds, he tried to take mine. So I filled his prescription bottles with placebos. It is not easy to find candy that resembles pills. He would fill his pill container and take them whenever he wanted to. I would give him the real pills later in the morning, and he took them without a hassle. Eventually I was able to confiscate his "pill" container and he didn't notice. Another problem solved!

But the worst *last* was his *last* voluntary shower which impacted me, all who visited and those poor clothes he wore. I tried every trick I knew to get him to bathe, even offering to shower with him. Eventually I imposed on Todd once a week to get him clean. There would be agitated shouting and swearing, and finally Todd said that he couldn't go through the anguish anymore. He simply said that Fred was his father and he didn't want those negative scenes to be his last memory of him. I understood. I hired some home health care workers. Some were successful; others weren't. I didn't realize that it was possible for a person to go so long without bathing.

During this time my daughter Allison was pregnant, and she was extremely sensitive to offensive odors. Since I lived with one, she found it difficult to visit us. I can remember her complaining that the couch on which Fred spent a greater part of his day reclining, smelled and that I should get rid of it. She would have preferred that I get rid of the source of the odor, but she loved this pungent smelly man.

▼

REMODELING

A chicken crossing the road is poultry in motion.

Some of my decisions during this trying time weren't the wisest. (See trip to Spain!) The one to have our main floor remodeled falls into this category. I had no control over Fred or our life together, and I desperately needed a project with a predictable beginning, middle, and end. So I decided to tear up our house and my husband's life. Poor Fred would come downstairs every morning to construction chaos. He would naturally begin swearing about what in the hell was going on. I did not foresee how difficult this break in his routine would be.

When the hardwood floors were being finished, I was told we were not to walk on them for 48 hours. I thought getting us out of the house would be the logical solution. Silly me! I packed a bag, got Mr. Grumps in the car and drove to Pueblo, where he had lived as a boy. I suggested that we spend the night there. This was as well received as if I had suggested we camped out in the Arctic.

"Why in the hell would we want to stay here?"

So I headed toward Denver, paused in Colorado Springs and said brightly, "Let's stay here for the night."

This idea was rejected with much vigor. I decided a change of tactics was in order. I simply would not give him a choice. I drove into the Best Western in Denver and said, "I'll check us in if you'll get the bag." I won't tell you what he said, but I did drive home. Before we got out of the car, I cautioned him to take off his shoes and to take just one step on the wood entry way before stepping on the carpeted stairs. So he went in with his grimy shoes on, walked around on the gleaming floors before retiring. I knew I deserved this punishment, but that didn't ease my rage.

One of the new remodeled kitchen features was glass cabinet doors behind which I proudly displayed matching dishes. Wooden doors hid everyday stuff: canned goods, boxes, and jars of food. When I put his beloved Banana Nut Crunch Cereal or his potato chips in the proper cabinet, it would drive Fred crazy because he couldn't find them. When he left them on the counter or put them behind my prized glass cabinets, it would drive me crazy. So that's why we began storing his cereal and potato chips in the refrigerator. *Problems with abstract thinking is number 6 in Alzheimer's 10 Warning Signs.*

In all fairness to Fred, my destroying and restoring the major part of our main floor was a dirty trick to pull on him. In my naiveté and denial, I didn't think the construction would make that much difference to him. How wrong I was!

Looking back, I can see how devastating it must have been for him. I didn't take into consideration how much his repetitious routine meant to him. I disturbed his daily schedule by stripping him of his familiar surroundings which were a comforting structure for him and placed him in areas that looked like a hurricane had whipped through taking everything but the plywood floors with it. Living with the dust and debris of remodeling is difficult for everyone involved, but it must have been a personal hell for him.

Here I was again in the grief stages of denial and bargaining. Thinking that Fred was oblivious to what was going on anyway, what could more confusion hurt? *Fred, I thought I was taking your welfare into consideration at all times, but I dropped the ball on this one, and for this I am truly sorry.*

Finally the restoration of the house was complete. I wish I could say that we were back to normal, but I had lost the meaning of that word. We had a new kitchen, family room, and dining room, but the worse for the wear was Fred. He never appreciated the updating I did to his surroundings, but I'm certain his life was easier when it was over.

CHAPTER ELEVEN

▼

GETTING SOBER

*A man walks into a bar with a slab
of concrete under his arm and says, "A
beer for me and one for the road."*

I've described a pathetic picture of poor ol' me and
what I had to put up with. I had a little help then from
and later a lot of help from my friend, Carlo Rossi, who
appeared on the label of my white wine of choice. I
will not blame Fred for my drinking a little and later a
lot of wine. I poured each glass of my own free will. It
was late June, 2001 when my three daughters and my

friend Marje confronted me with my drinking. They gave me three choices (or so I thought.) :   quit on my own; return to AA, or go into rehab. In their minds only the third option was acceptable.

I chose door number one to which I got this response, "Mother, you've tried many times to quit and you haven't stuck with it."

"OK, door number two."

"Mother, you have been to AA before and that didn't work."

I certainly did not like the third alternative, but they already had a reserved a place for me in Parker Valley Hope Rehabilitation Center. They took me home to pack. I tried to explain to Fred where I was going and why. He followed me like a puppy back and forth from my closet to my suitcase as I threw things in.

He kept saying, "Patricia, you don't have to go. You can stay here." I knew if I listened to him that I would stay home. Clearly, he was afraid; I was too.

I continued to repeat, "I have to go. You can come see me. Todd will come take you to dinner every day. I'll talk to you on the phone every day. The girls will check on you. Fred, I have to go."

Each daughter brought Fred to visit me at Parker Valley, but he wasn't comfortable there and didn't want to stay. However, he always wanted me to come home with him and couldn't understand why I wouldn't come. Fortunately we both made it through that month that seemed to last a year. I then went to the prescribed ninety AA meetings in ninety days and became a healthier person. I wish I could say the same for Fred, but he was at least happier that I was home. I could quit drinking, but he couldn't quit toting the monkey on his back.

While I was in the rehabilitation center, there were group therapy sessions and individual counseling sessions. For me the common occurrence of all of them was to be asked what was I going to do differently so I wouldn't drink when I got home. Everyone concerned seemed convinced that once I was home with my friend Fred that I would go back to my next best friend, Wine. But miraculously I did not. While I may have been tempted a time or two, I would be kidding myself if I ever did drink and blame it on Fred. I could blame countless inconveniences on him, but my alcohol consumption was my very own STUPID choice.

It's my belief that we all have our baggage to carry and most people survive their past without too many scars. I dislike the term, "dysfunctional family," because of its overuse. What family functions like the ones in the sitcoms where the biggest problems can be solved in less than a half hour with humor? Because I was raised in a home with a loving, but alcoholic mother and a distant workaholic father, my expectations of family life may have been lowered a notch or two. This may have been a blessing. Possibly living with demented Fred was easier because of my past. As Fred would have said, "No one knows, but the Shadow." (And he said that often!)

▼

Chapter Twelve

Laurie

He had a photographic memory
which was never developed.

Fred's Alzheimer's had a devastating impact on his daughter, Laurie. She adored him as a person, relied on him as a friend, and loved him as her father. When I asked her to write down some of her memories of her dad before and after he changed so drastically, she was thrilled that I was writing about him, but hesitated to put her feelings on paper. Once she began sharing her recollections, it was like opening the flood gates.

She shared that her dad was a wonderful father with whom she could share her most intimate thoughts, things that normally a girl would only share with her mother. "Dad would always listen, offer me advice, comfort and guidance, but rarely told me what to do."

However, she recalled an exception when he did tell her what to do. She believes his urging led her to marry Bob, her husband of nineteen years. They had broken up after going together for three years. Bob had gone to Michigan to be with his ailing father. Laurie flew there from Colorado to determine if there was anything left of their relationship. When Bob couldn't commit to any future, she left, telling him never to call her again. Heartbroken, she sobbed to her dad how much she missed Bob and how desperately she wanted to call him. This wise father told her not to call him, but to give Bob time to miss her. After a week, Bob asked her to return and be with him for his dad's funeral. He then told her how much he missed her and proposed marriage. They got married in Denver that year. To this day, Laurie is thankful for her dad's sage advice.

A funny thing happened on Fred's way to his church pew after giving away his daughter. He sat down beside the wrong wife! After walking Laurie down the aisle, he was supposed to sit by Carolyn, the bride's mother. Instead he plopped down by Carol, his second wife, who happened to be sitting right behind Carolyn. When he discovered his mistake, he waited until the guests stood to sing a hymn, and discreetly slipped up to the first row next to the correct wife. I would have loved to have been there just to witness such a faux pas, but that would have further complicated an already complicated scene.

When Laurie and Bob moved to Michigan as man and wife, her only regret was leaving her best friend, her father. But Fred called her every weekend until Mr. Alzheimer's interfered. "I wish I could remember his last phone call. Had I known it would be the last I would have treasured that call and remembered every detail." Of course, she would call him, but it wasn't the same. Eventually when she called, he would hand the phone to me, either because he did not know who she was or he did not know what to say to her.

"Dad was the best father and mother a girl could have. It was he who came to be with me when my children were born." She explained that baby Jennifer, her first born, arrived prematurely and was too small to go home with her. Laurie was so distraught that Fred flew out early to be with her. She remembers him being so loving and gentle with this tiny baby. She was very grateful that her father was eager to come and help her. "Normally that is something a mother should do. He knew my mom wouldn't so he did. I also think he just wanted to."

Laurie's first inkling that her dad was having significant problems is the last time he drove to Michigan for a visit. He loved long car trips and had big plans of seeing the country on the way there and back. He called Laurie on my cell phone (which I had insisted he take for the following reason) when he thought he was close to the Storie's house to get specific directions. Laurie had a difficult time trying to figure out where he was. He wasn't close at all and was getting farther away with each minute because he was going in the wrong direction. She got a map so she could follow him as he turned around. He read highway numbers and street names to her as he progressed toward their home.

She didn't dare let him hang up for fear he would get lost again. Finally, after more than an hour of her coaching, he arrived, worn out and a bit shaken. (A side note: when I received my cell phone bill the next month, I too was a bit shaken with the tab of $132 which normally was around $20!)

Bob's mother, Ann, had been diagnosed with Alzheimer's. Fred and Laurie were visiting on her living room couch when he spotted a pamphlet listing the symptoms of this disease on the coffee table. In a frightened voice he read the items one by one saying, "I do that" and "I do that." He was as close to crying as Laurie had seen in many years. She reports that they "both knew in their hearts that he had fallen prey to this terrible disease." By the time he was ready to drive home, he had abandoned all thoughts of extending his trip for sightseeing.

A most disappointing episode for her occurred on her next trip to visit us in Denver. She wanted to surprise her dad so she had her brother Todd pick her up at Denver International Airport. They drove to our house, and Todd came into our family room with a big smile on his face.

He announced to his dad, "Do I have a surprise for you!"

Laurie walked in, and she could tell immediately that he had no idea who she was. And he reinforced this feeling when he said in his generic greeting, "Why, how are you? I haven't seen you in a long time." These words might have been fine from another father to another daughter, but they were a dead giveaway in this case.

"He would always give me money if he knew I needed it. I would not even have to ask." She laments how the dementia made a tightwad of her generous dad. "That was something I found so sad about Alzheimer's. It took away the man I had known and loved. I remember testing him one day. I wanted to see if he would part with any of his money because he had become so cheap. I asked him if I could have a penny. He firmly told me, 'No, I don't have any money.' "

My daughter Allison spent more time with Fred than my other two daughters because she lived at home with us some of the time. She agrees with Laurie that she could talk to Fred about anything. She talked to him about college choices and education in general. Because he seemed to have a wide knowledge in these areas, she remembers being surprised that he was an accountant. She had thought he would have been in education or some social service position. She recalls he suggested that she work on a cruise ship after she graduated from the University of Colorado, an appealing idea to this open young student.

And she remembers his humor. When she asked him if he had just had a haircut, he replied, "No, I got all of them cut." She didn't even groan, but she always asked him this when she noticed his hair had been trimmed so she could get his absurd answer.

When I quizzed Lora, who has cleaned my house twice a month for over twenty five years what her remembrances of Fred were, she reminded me that she also cleaned Fred's condo while we were dating. She said she was always impressed by how neat Fred's place was. She was a witness to his deterioration over the years. She recalled a time when we had just returned from some trip. She asked Fred how the trip was. Predictably he said, "Fine." She then asked where we went. It startled her a bit when he answered that he didn't know. He said, "It's a good thing Patricia takes pictures so I can find out where we've been."

▼

CHAPTER THIRTEEN

JAIL

When you've seen one shopping
center, you've seen a mall.

One more Banana Nut Crunch story! His son and I knew that we should take Fred's car away, but it seemed too cruel to rob him of his freedom. I told myself that he only drove short distances to the store and occasionally to the gas station. He was a deliberate and slow driver. One day he was gone longer than usual so I went to look for him. There was no sign of his car in the lot in front of King Soopers. I then drove to Safeway. I was relieved to see his vintage Cadillac in the parking lot. After searching all the aisles for him, I asked the check-out clerk to page him. His worried look worried me, especially when he pointed to Fred's car and asked me if it was my husband's. He mumbled something about trouble and called the manager. She explained that they had watched Fred for over a long period of time walking out of the store with milk and cereal without paying. When confronted, he would act as though he had forgotten and would politely hand over the money. This day he became belligerent, the store called the police, and out of anger or fear or both, Fred pushed the officer. I paled at the thought of his being in jail.

Shaking with anxiety, I called the Arapahoe County Justice Center and was told I would need to bring a cashier's check of $5000.00 bond to get this dangerous criminal who shoplifted a box of cereal released. I went to my bank to get the check and raced to the center. Check in hand, I walked into the justice center. It was quite familiar to me because I formerly had been a volunteer in their jail library. I knew where to lock my purse, but I didn't know where my poor husband was.

I gave the check to the receptionist and asked if she would release Fred. I wanted to strangle her when she calmly said that the cashier's check had to be in Fred's name, not mine. I grabbed the check, broke a few ordinances of my own while speeding to Fred's bank, and returned to the jail. When I thrust down the new check, the same lady instructed me to sit in the waiting room for it would be anywhere from two to five hours before he would be released. I controlled my inward hysteria and explained that Fred had Alzheimer's and this ordeal would be painfully confusing for him. Fortunately for her (or I might have landed in a cell myself), she passed this information to an officer and told me to take a seat. With unfocused eyes, I stared at a magazine for what seemed like an eternity, but it was only minutes until my gentleman jailbird came strolling out. He was carrying a paper sack, containing his billfold, his belt, and his *underwear*! I could have cried!

We walked out to freedom together, and as I glanced back at this towering edifice behind us, I asked Fred, "Was that just awful for you?"

He answered, "What did we do, have a pacemaker check-up?"

For the first and last time, I was grateful for his total lack of memory. On the way home I stopped at a different store to pick up milk and Banana Nut Crunch. (For all the free plugs I've given this cereal, Post should consider donating heavily to the Alzheimer's Association.)

The next day, we had to appear in court. Todd, his attorney son, who had defended many people in this court before, was now representing his father. We were asked to stand when the judge entered the courtroom; Fred refused to budge. When we sat down, Fred stood up. When the judge heard the case, it was dismissed immediately.

We received the bond money back in the form of a check. Before I could deposit it in Fred's account, once again we were at our favorite haunt, the super market. While we waited in line to pay for our groceries, I noticed Fred counting his money. He was carrying around $5000.00 in cash! I was aghast. But the more I thought about it, as tight as he was with a dollar, the money was probably safer with him than in a bank.

CHAPTER FOURTEEN

MORE TRICKS

Did you hear the one about the guy whose whole left side was cut off? He's all right now.

"Some time in the middle of the night, I'm going to drive down here and pull out all of these ---- stop signs." This quote of Fred's doesn't require a lot of explanation except that stop signs annoyed him as did all disruptions to his life. Fortunately, he never followed through with this drastic threat. Since he thought this was a brand new solution to this problem, he would repeat this every time I stopped at an offensive stop sign. To me it was as irritating as being cut off on the phone to "If you'd like to make a call, please hang up and dial again." After hearing his preposterous comment for the umpteenth time, you'd think I could anticipate it with ease. Wrong! Wrong! Wrong! Many a time I seriously considered running the STUPID sign to avoid the inevitable threat.

King Soopers' employees informed me that Fred had also been shoplifting there, not only milk and Banana Nut Crunch, but quantities of candy bars as well. I had to watch him like a toddler when I took him to the store. I would be ready to pay for my groceries, and the clerk would ask me if I also wanted to pay for the candy in Fred's jacket.

He also must have escaped without paying for his gasoline a time or two because he confessed that at a particular station, the attendant would come out glaring at him with his hands on his hips as Fred was filling up. He must have pushed the *Pay Inside* button, put his gas in, and drove off a time or two. In fact, one day he confided to Allison's husband, Tom ,his great secret. He told him that if he wanted to get free gas, there was a station nearby where he could fill up and leave. He may have had Alzheimer's disease, but the conniving, problem solving area of his brain was still working. Sadly, the ethical part wasn't.

One day Todd and I tried to convince him to get his prescriptions filled at Dr. Lazeroff's clinic. We told them that it was just as economical to get them filled there as anywhere else. Fred argued that he knew of a place that was much cheaper. Todd asked him where that would be.

Fred answered, "King Soopers. You just go in, give them the prescription, walk around until it's ready, pick it up, put it inside your jacket, and walk out."

Todd was outraged. "Dad, that's shoplifting. You can't do that."

Fred responded, "I don't care what you call it. It's cheaper than at this blankety blank place."

Fred loved Cadillacs although even in his sane life, he was too frugal to buy a new one. He had driven a series of previously owned ones which were in good condition.

The salesmen at a local Cadillac dealership were, of course, as friendly and welcoming as all competent sales people. Fred enjoyed their company (which I think he mistook for friendship) and their cars. I'm not saying they took advantage of him, but when he came home after purchasing a model older than the one he drove in with, I question if they had his best interest at heart.

Finally his son and I made the long overdue decision to confiscate the thief's car. Todd drove it to Cadillac heaven, a car lot filled with similar vintage autos. Amazingly Fred did not ask about his missing car nor did he attempt to drive my car. All our worry and concern about taking away his independence and his manhood was for naught.

But the mischief wasn't over. He was zealous about having items returned to their proper place. And obviously the proper place was our kitchen counter. He would return from a walk around the block like a proud birddog toting his prey and deposit: a child's coat, various toys left on lawns, a watch, and so much loot, I could have opened a second hand store. Instead I put plea in our homeowner's newsletter entitled *Found*. And then there was the day a bag of groceries appeared on our kitchen counter. Apparently, either he found them in the back seat of a car (groceries don't belong there; they belong in our kitchen) or perhaps they were left on some porch for a charity pick up. Well, my charity case picked them up!

Our house backed up to a greenbelt area that contained an Olympic size swimming pool and several tennis courts. Frequently there were stray yellow tennis balls hidden like Easter eggs in the flower beds, bushes, and grassy lawn. Fred would collect these treasures as if they had been placed there for his pleasure. He would fill his jacket with these lost balls and put them in the repository for all found items, our kitchen counter. Returning them to courts became routine for me. I only wished I could have returned all the other found prizes as easily.

When life was beginning to offer little meaning for Fred, I found the Johnson Adult Day Care Center which seemed to be the answer. I hoped it would give him some needed stimulation and me some freedom. (By then I had retired from my position at the church.) They served the participants coffee and juice around a big round table and discussed the daily newspaper, not that Fred ever read the paper except the comics. (Also he would work on the word searches on the Children's Page. He was very proud when he completed one.) The Johnson Center had exercises for the body and the deteriorating mind. The caregivers would even give him a needed shower! I made arrangements to take him there twice a week. He never settled into the routine and stood on the periphery of all activities.

Apparently he was his obstinate self there also. The director told me that unless he was on some medication to allow him to be more cooperative, she would have to terminate his visits. She also gave me some advice which I thought was rather drastic at the time, but I wish I had taken to heart. She told me if Fred were her father she would put him in a psychiatric hospital for a couple of months to accurately assess what medications he needed. That sounded like overkill and expensive to me. I must admit I often shared Fred's thrifty gene. But if I had it to do all over, I would do just that. Instead, I just quit taking him to the adult day care center.

Most of our neighbors were understanding of his condition, but I received more than a few calls complaining about my wanderer's behavior. Specifically, people didn't like Fred looking through their mail. During this time, a bomb placed in a mailbox had exploded somewhere in the Midwest. The Post Office officials asked that all mailboxes be left open. The crisis passed; the culprit was caught, and mailboxes could be closed. But how could Fred see what was inside if they were closed? So when he went on his several times a day walks around the block, he would open all the mailboxes which were located near the sidewalk. If the contents looked interesting, he would rifle through them. On more than one occasion, I would find other homeowners' mail mixed in with ours. Returning the items wasn't always pleasant. I asked our mailperson if Fred was breaking a federal law, by tampering with the United States mail.

She said, "No, I've talked to Fred many times. I know what you're dealing with."

Funny, I didn't!

Dr. Lazeroff had warned me that so far Fred merely walked around the block, but that could change on any walk. "Fred will see something that intrigues him across the street and continue around that block. He won't have any idea where he is and could wander away without any means of getting home." I ordered him an identification bracelet with the Alzheimer's logo, his ID number, and a telephone number to call, but he refused to wear it.

The most difficult decision I have ever had to make was deciding to place Fred in a locked facility. I knew he and I were living on borrowed time. I couldn't keep him in the house, and one day my luck and his would run out. A friend recommended a lady whose business was locating and securing the most appropriate placement for her needy geriatric clients. With relief, I hired her. She advised us to visit a delightful home near a lake which had several bedrooms for people with special needs. After the affable manager interviewed Fred, he thought my husband might be too great a risk for his place.

"Fine!" I thought. "I'll just take my risk home."

Next we visited a young couple with a home similar to ours in a nearby neighborhood. I could see Fred living there although I was concerned by their security. The simple lock on the front door looked too easy to crack by my devious darling. But the couple was so positive and reassuring that Fred would fit in with the other residents that I accepted their offer.

My dear friend Marje and I drove over to Dr. Lazeroff's house to get his signature on the application. He looked sad as he signed the papers. When he handed the papers to me, his demeanor was one of a resigned, tired man. He didn't say anything, but I read into his body language, "Another one of my poor patients warehoused."

When we got back into the car, I was devastated. I broke down crying as if I had lost my beloved forever.

Marje asked me directly, "What do you really want to do?"

"I want to keep him at home," I sobbed.

"Well, why don't you?"

Immediate relief and a wave of happiness washed over me. I went home, grabbed the phone and cancelled the previously made arrangements. Fred didn't improve any; nor did I in my care of him. But I felt more resolve that I could handle him at home. I knew in my heart he would be much better off and far happier. Months went by and I didn't regret my decision to keep Fred with me.

However, my daughters were concerned that he could harm me or their children for whom I often babysat. He had little control of his temper. By then my grandchildren had increased to the number eight. One or two or more could be underfoot on most any day. Fred often napped on the family room couch, the center of activity.

One day when toddler Andy innocently woke him up, startled Fred began shouting and raised his arm to strike this little intruder. That's all it took. I couldn't take any more chances with the outbreaks of this unpredictable man with these vulnerable children around. *Rapid changes in mood and behavior is number 8 in the warning sign list.*

CHAPTER FIFTEEN

CONFINEMENT

*Mahatma Gandhi walked barefoot most
of the time which produced an impressive
set of calluses on his feet. He was frail
because he ate so little. His odd diet gave
him bad breath. This made him a Super-
calloused fragile mystic hexed by halitosis.*

Even though intellectually I had made the decision to
find a place for Fred where he would be safe, well
cared for, and hopefully happy, emotionally I was still
struggling. One minute I would be ready to pack his

bags and next one, I felt relief that he was sleeping on the couch. I made endless lists of the pros and cons of moving him out. Here is a sample which I wrote during this time of indecision.

The Pros of His Moving

My safety:

He raises his fist likes he's going to hit me.

He acts like he's going to stab me.

He hits me on the head with a rolled up newspaper.

He pretends to choke me.

He loses his temper when he's corrected.

(Let it be known that Fred never touched me in anger, but since he was almost a foot taller than I and weighed almost twice as much, this "play acting" of his could be intimidating. And his behavior worried my daughters.)

The grandchildren:

He swears in front of them.

He gets angry when they are here.

I'm afraid he will lose his temper and hurt one of them.

He irritates them when they are playing or eating.
They loved this man, but now were becoming fearful
of him.

His hygiene:

He won't shower. We're going on week four. Todd has
not been able to get him into the shower the last two
times he's tried. He swears and yells at Todd.
He smells bad.
The couch smells bad.
His hair needs washing.
He leaks urine.

His medications:

Even though I try to control them, he finds them and
takes too many.
He takes my medications.

The house:

He thaws food, only to place it in a cabinet where it
spoils.
He puts dirty dishes and silverware away.
He won't flush toilets; the house smells bad.
He turns up the heat, even in the summer.

He spits on the porches and garage floor, staining both.

The dog:

He kicks my Chihuahua, Rufus, when he gets in his way.

He overfeeds him and gives him table food making Rufus happy but fat.

My sister Michelle added two more in her handwriting:

He's ruining the couch.

He answers the phone, but forgets to deliver the messages.

Michelle usually visited us twice a year so she knew our situation well. We would often discuss the pros and cons of Fred staying home versus going into an assisted living arrangement.   One of her main concerns was the sanitation aspect of our dishes. Fred would drink a cup of coffee, wipe it out with a dishtowel, and put in back in the cupboard. Or he would polish off a bowl of cereal, and wipe it out with the same dry cloth. I had a habit of inspecting all dishes and pieces of silverware before I used them so I became rather blasé about this practice. As a guest, Michelle was shocked at the thought of dirty dishes mingled with the clean ones. She was not amused when I called her "picky."

Taken individually, most of these "pros" seem solvable. But collectively, they were overwhelmingly convincing that I needed to take some action. Of course, the only "con" to moving him out of our home was also powerful. I dearly loved this man, warts, Alzheimer's and all.

I had visited a care center specializing in memory loss patients, a poorly disguised euphemism for Alzheimer's disease. I was most impressed with the orderly, modern yet homey atmosphere. The overly exuberant administrator gave me a tour and assured me of its security and of their familiarity with residents like Fred. It sounded perfect, especially the part that they could handle my wayward husband.

Michelle flew in from Texas to help me with the move. We carefully decorated his pleasant private room with his family photographs on the walls, rugs on the hardwood floor, his television set on his dresser, and all personal affects we thought would make him feel comfortable.

Finally the time arrived. We had no trouble getting him into the car and once we were in the center's cheerful waiting room, one of the caretakers distracted him while Michelle and I slipped out. A red flag should have waved when the administrator advised me not to visit him for several days until he had enough time to adjust to his new home. But she was the professional who knew about these things so I readily accepted her recommendation without question. (Even though I disagree with this practice, I have since realized that it is widely used.) I felt guilty in how relieved and relaxed I felt now that a team was dealing with him and just not me. How comforting to know that he was going to be clean, well fed, safe, and I was hoping I could add *happy* to that list.

During the afternoon of day two, Fred attempted an escape out the front door. Why was I not even a little bit surprised? When several employees tried to coax him back to his room, he exploded into verbal and physical violence. No one could safely get near him so they called 911. He was transported to a hospital on the other side of town. I don't know how he was restrained or if he went in an ambulance or police car. I didn't want to know.

By the time I could get to the other side of the city of Denver to this hospital, I found him drugged into oblivion. The psychiatric nurse in charge, Char, turned out to be a much loved and respected choir member of our church. I didn't know her well at the time, but I felt somewhat better when she told me that Alzheimer's patients were her favorites.   But it was devastating leaving him there. This was an old drab building, and to be brutally honest, was filled with old, drab people. Actually they were very troubled people.

For two weeks his son and I visited this zombie daily. When I asked about the possibility of his being over medicated, I was assured that it was to keep him calm and that they would be gradually lessen these meds. Usually I would find him unresponsive or asleep in a wheel chair when I came to see him. Occasionally I found him in isolation as a consequence of his acting out, and I would feel sick at heart for him, but strangely pleased that he still had enough spunk to get into trouble.

One day my daughter Allison went with me to visit him. We walked down these 1950's grim institutional halls until we came upon a sign announcing *Geriatric Psychiatric Patients* with an arrow pointing to a locked door. Allison quipped, "Yep, we have one of those." Indeed we did.

Eventually, I received a call informing me that Fred could be released. But there was a hitch. He was not allowed to return to his care center. It seems they were only prepared to handle docile memory loss patients. In fact, Fred had been labeled a behavior problem, and only three places in the entire metropolitan area of greater Denver would be able to take him. One had a fairly good reputation, but it was about 50 miles outside of town. The other one was in a stark hospital setting and the only place for him to go outside was a small concrete patio with no shade. The third place was one I had visited a year ago because Jan (who was on our Panama Canal trip) said that it was a wonderful place for her mother. This place struck my friend Marje and me as old, dreary and depressing.

When we toured the area, one of the male residents clutched my arm hanging on for dear life. Since he wouldn't let me go, he accompanied us throughout his unit. I made some smart aleck remark that I wouldn't put my worst enemy there. I humbly ate those words after both Char and Dr. Lazeroff said it was staffed with knowledgeable personnel and Fred would be well cared for there.

Since the center with the upbeat designer environment couldn't accommodate him, could it be possible that a place's appearance was merely comforting for the loved ones who come to visit, but not an indication of the quality of care? This new center had four separate sections of patients based on the individual's capabilities: assisted living for the highly functioning; nursing care residents who were continent; incontinent nursing care persons, and the last was reserved for those with behavior problems. This unit was commonly known as the *bad boys*. Naturally Fred was placed in the latter. In fact, the man who had held my arm a year ago was still there, but fortunately showed no interest in escorting me.

I had no choice. Fred would be delivered from the hospital to his new home. Once again before he arrived, I tried to make his side of the room personal and welcoming (no private room here!). However, the light was dawning. I was going to this trouble so *I* would feel welcome. I hung his drop-dead handsome portrait an old girlfriend painted of him when he was in his twenties over his bed. (I swear it was a young Kirk Douglas, complete with rugged face and dimpled chin.) I brought in a rug to match his bedspread and throw pillows for his half a room he shared with someone who was never there. Later I realized my decorating skills were totally unnecessary here. The bedspread and pillows disappeared quickly, and the rug was rolled up deemed to be a hazard for tripping.

I was notified when he arrived, and I immediately went to see him. We both sat down on his bed and were joined by two other men. One was practically sitting on my hip as the four of us sat like stone faced jurors staring at nothing. But I didn't dare want to disturb one of the bad boys by asking them to move over or to leave.

On subsequent visits, I discovered someone wearing Fred's golf shirt. At first I resented this. I had lost enough of Fred without also losing his clothes that represented the familiar man I loved. But when I found Fred was wearing someone's red jogging pants, several sizes too small, I complimented him on his new Capri pants. I tried to take this entire wardrobe sharing in stride until I found Fred's cramped feet in someone else's tennis shoes. I did complain and the staff made every effort to find Fred's size 12 shoes. My requirements for Fred's optimum daily life decreased as did his.

The residents not only shared clothes, but also food which was served in the dining room on individual trays. Often I would sit with Fred while he ate. He would start with his dessert and then nonchalantly reach over to another *bad boy's* tray and finish his.

A common game the attendants and I often played was called "Where was Fred?" I never saw him sleeping on or in his own bed. When I came to see him, I would check his empty room first, then the television area, the game room, and finally I would ask an employee for help. Then a paraprofessional and I would go from room to room checking beds. The winner was the one who found him napping on someone else's bed; the prize, Fred!

The complex was built in a square around a lovely large lawn with mature shade trees, swings and picnic tables. This was by far the best feature of the place and one Fred and I frequented every daily visit I made. We'd walk around it, often holding hands like a normal couple taking a stroll. Often I'd sing some of the old songs we used to sing together, hoping he, who had the great voice, would join me. But he would not. I probably wouldn't have joined me either.

Once I got him to help me rake the colorful leaves and occasionally we would swing on the glider. At first he would try to leave with me, but then an attendant would catch his attention while I guiltily sneaked out.

▼

CHAPTER SIXTEEN

FAREWELL

A will is a dead giveaway

For the most part, I felt that Fred was well cared for in this rather depressing nursing home. The downside was that he was surrounded with patients like himself who could not provide any care, interest or stimulation. The professional and lay staff seemed competent and invested in the well being of the residents. Even though Fred had only lived there less than three months, some of the attendants seemed particularly fond of him. I was impressed with the number of caretakers who worked during the week. However, on weekends there seemed to be less staff, and certainly fewer doctors and professionals were around.

One Saturday in November, 2003, I came into the facility expecting to look for Fred, find him, and visit him with no special expectations. After searching in a few rooms, I found him in a strange bed with only his underwear on. He was restless, unresponsive, and appeared feverish. I quickly summoned the male nurse in charge who was only filling in for the day. He called Fred's doctor. An aide and I tried to get him to drink some water, but with no success. His doctor came and gave him an antibiotic, but Fred's body would not rally. All the residents had had flu shots earlier, but several had come down with the virus anyway. Fred's infection turned into pneumonia. I believe that he had no will to live or spirit to fight for his life. He, who did not know what was going on in his world, certainly could not battle a threatening illness.

I called Laurie in Michigan and Todd to tell them the severity of his condition. Todd was able to visit his dad before he died although he was lying peaceful in a coma. Laurie, to her great disappointment, did not arrive in time. Years earlier, she had been summoned to come to say goodbye to Grandma Lu, and we all called it a miracle because only minutes after Laurie arrived at her bed, Lula left this world. Laurie was deeply saddened that her beloved father could not wait for her. Possibly he wanted to spare her from seeing him so incapacitated.

When Fred died, I thought that my grief would not be as profound as what I had experienced so often in the past five years. I had mourned over Fred's deterioration for so long that I thought I was prepared for his death. I had convinced myself that he would be better off in heaven with his mother, father, sister and brother. Or if that comforting thought did not pan out, then at least he was no longer living in a world that had become so confusing and frightening. The *Real* Fred had been such a participant and appreciator of life that it seemed unusually cruel to have had his body going through motions without his awareness. But even with all my preparedness, the finality of his demise was staggering.

Fred followed his father's footsteps rather than his religious mother's. He refused to attend church although he confessed to believing in a higher power. I managed to get him to enter God's house for most of the grandchildren's baptisms, some weddings, and Lula's funeral. So for him a church service almost seemed inappropriate. But, right or wrong, I decided that for those who loved him, a final service for tribute and good-bye was necessary.

Fred had had definite opinions about most important issues, but I remember complete avoidance on the subject of what he wanted to be done with his body. His children and I decided on cremation because we felt that this was in keeping with the Fred we knew. The Monarch Society attended to that task and delivered his remains to Wellshire Presbyterian Church's Memorial Garden where he was interred. Now I could always find him in a peaceful setting. He would be only minutes from my home, insuring no chance of his getting lost. There were enough ashes left over to divide among Todd, Laurie, and me. To this day I have my portion in a vase on the mantel in my living room. I don't announce this fact to visitors so please don't mention this to anyone. At last I can finally keep my eye on him.

After talking with Todd, Laurie, and me about the essence of Fred, Reverend Robert Ward delivered a sensitive remembrance of him. Often pastors use a memorial service as an occasion to preach the Word. This would have been out of line for Fred's service, and I was thankful that Robert did not. The service was short and simple; I think Fred would have approved.

My sisters, Michelle and Peggy, her husband Dale, and daughter Andrea came from Texas. Bob, Laurie, Jennifer, and Tyler arrived from Michigan. Todd and Sue as well as my children and grandchildren were among the mourners who attended. His nieces and nephew and their children came from Pueblo, plus there were a smattering of his friends, our friends and my friends.

It was a bittersweet farewell because the Fred taken by death was not the Fred those in attendance knew and loved. We were remembering and grieving the vibrant, irreverent, fun loving Fred Thompson who had embraced and loved life who left us long ago. It was tragic enough that he died an early death at age seventy three. But the tragedy was doubled when he lost his life in stages, first his mind and then his body.

▼

CHAPTER SEVENTEEN

LIFE AFTER FRED

A backward poet writes inverse.

Even today I am continually reminded of Fred, and it's been over six years since he left this world . Spotting a handsome grey haired man with his stature sends me into a panic mode. Suddenly I feel as if I have found my long lost love only to lose him again when I realize this is not my handsome grey haired man. Finding even the smallest memento of his takes me back to the day he died. Years after his death, I was cleaning my desk and found his comical business card he had given me when we were first dating. Under **Fred W. Thompson** were listed his areas of expertise: Wars Fought, Uprisings Quelled, Governments Run, Tigers Tamed, Bars Emptied, Virgins Deflowered, Wild Parties Crashed, Orgies Organized, Troubles Listened to, and Backs Rubbed. Of course, this was a huge exaggeration. I know for a fact he never tamed a tiger.

I was able to dispose of his things in a fairly efficient manner due to a variety of factors:

a.) He had pared down his belongings every time he started over in a new household.

b.) Todd and Laurie divided all of the personal items of his that they wanted.

c.) giving the dozens of golf shirts to Goodwill was not a difficult decision.

I was surprised when the Salvation Army said they would pick up his mammoth desk because Todd had to break it apart to get it out of Fred's office. I kept the credenza in which he had stored the returns of all his clients for whom he did taxes. I keep my personal current papers in this monster file which is a constant reminder of him. I sometimes smile at this bulky piece of furniture, and I sometimes frown. This is good because that's in keeping with my reaction to its previous owner.

I have a photographic record of us as a couple that goes back to one of our first dates. It warms my heart when I thumb through the many scrapbooks I've kept containing our various trips, our family gatherings, and small details of our life together. I look at this handsome man carrying one of the babies, playing with a toddler, or just holding my hand, and I want to scream at the unfairness. Just as often it makes me sad to realize how happy we were and could have been today had it not been for the destruction caused by the plaques and tangles of Alzheimer's.

I still have a few journal writings about our life together which all too often are filled with the facts of our activities, not the good or bad feelings. I try to revive the emotions as I read the entries. I admonish myself for writing like a journalistic reporter instead of a memoirist. Currently, I am teaching a memoir writing class at Osher Lifelong Learning Institute, an adult education program sponsored by the University of Denver. I vehemently plead with my students to include the joy, pain, and fear as well as their anecdotal entries.

Do as I say, not as I did.

This chapter is devoted to life after Fred which contains painful and heartwarming memories. I asked my sister Michelle who visited us once or twice a year what she remembers most about Fred. She remembers his humor, kindness, and good looks, but unfortunately, she recalls more of his later life. She said he scared her to death when she stayed with us in the basement guest room. He would creep downstairs, peak around the door like a jack-in-the-box, and disappear once he saw her. I told her I knew that game well. Although she knew it was Fred, he always startled her. To feel safe, she would pile her suitcases and a chair against the bedroom door so he couldn't open it. What kind of spoil sport she turned out to be!

My sister Peggy brought to my attention one of the expressions he used all too often. When anyone thanked him, me, or anyone in his presence, he would mimic a pathetic impersonation of Elvis. He would stammer,

"Th-Th Thank you very much." in his deep quasi Presley voice. How could I have forgotten that old standby? No doubt this was buried in my subconscious along with countless other gems.

One of these gems was that he would sing "Michael, Row Your Boat Ashore" when he heard Michelle's name, (She pronounces it *Michael*). She also reminded me with his obsession with the time of day. He insisted that all the clocks had to be in sync, a real challenge for a three story house with numerous time pieces. The microwave and oven time dials threw him in a dither. One would turn into the next number three or so seconds before the other. And her Texas car clock being an hour ahead of Colorado time truly baffled him.

She recalls his repeatedly bringing in a bunch of grapes from the backyard vines and asking her, "Have you ever seen grapes like these?" She thought it too rude to answer, "Yes, I did just a few minutes ago when you brought that last bunch in."

But I think it was the constant running commentary on the gas prices that almost drove her back to Texas.

"There's $1.95 on that corner and a $1.97 over there." To this day, whenever I hear someone comment on the price of gas, I don't know whether to laugh or cry.

I'm reluctant to end this writing because by closing, it will somehow mean I'm ending my connection to Fred. And I never want to do that. I will treasure the totality of my friend, lover, and husband named Fred. I will cherish the memory of this bright, witty, and well groomed man, while at the same time, have a great depth of feeling for the man he sadly became.

My hope for you, dear reader, is that when you visit your library or favorite book store in the near future and you inquire about memoirs about victims of Alzheimer's, the librarian will tell you since the disease has been eradicated, there is only a small collection available. I can't think of a better bequest to the memory of Fred Wilbur Thompson.